AF480173

THE UNHAPPY SOLAR SYSTEM

WRITTEN BY LORENE WALKER

ILLUSTRATED BY ADDISON GREEN

The Unhappy Solar System

Published by WalkersChildrensBooks, LLC, at lorenewalker60@gmail.com. Order a hardbound Premium Edition of this book at lorenewalker.com or order a print-on-demand or Kindle version at amazon.com.

ISBN: 978-1-915424-73-0

Dedication

The idea for this book emerged while helping my son prepare for a 1st grade assignment about our Solar System. While some students collaborated with a parent to create planetary dioramas and models, my son's submission was a short story of planetary facts as I worked with him to understand that the uniqueness and differences between the planets collectively determine what our Solar System truly represents.

At that time, his teacher encouraged further developing this theme as a children's book.

Twenty years later, after a good deal of refining, I'm excited to finally share this story. I believe it sends a powerful message on the importance of diversity.

This book is dedicated to my husband, Chris. A lifetime with you isn't enough.

- LW

One fine day, Mister Sun was looking at his nine beautiful planets all lined up in a row.

"They come in all different sizes and colors," said Mister Sun. "And I just *love them all*!"

But as Mister Sun looked more closely at his planets, he noticed they weren't so happy.

The planets were looking at each other and arguing back and forth. They had *frowns* on their faces!

"What seems to be the problem?" Mister Sun asked the planets.

All at once, the planets began shouting. It became *very loud*!

"Hold on! One at a time!" said Mister Sun.

"Ok, Mister Mercury, you begin first!" said Mister Sun. "Please tell me how you're feeling."

"I'm now the smallest planet, Mister Sun, and the other planets sometimes make fun of me because of my size. I'm also the planet closest to the sun, which hurts my eyes!

"To make things worse," continued Mister Mercury, "I have the most craters of any other planet in the Solar System. I don't like that because I don't want to look **rough and rugged**. Instead, I want to be **flatter and smoother**, like the other planets!

"I'm not as happy as I'd like to be," said Mister Mercury.

"Hmmm," Mister Sun mumbled with concern.

"Miss Venus, you're next," said Mister Sun. "Are you well?"

"No," said Miss Venus. "I'm the hottest planet in the Solar System and this makes me thirsty because my planet has no water. Also, my surface is covered by more volcanoes than any other planet. I don't like it when my volcanoes erupt. It gives me a **headache**!

"And why does my planet spin clockwise, the opposite of every other planet? I feel like I'm going in the **wrong direction**!

"I'm just so unhappy," said Miss Venus.

"OK, I hear you," said Mister Sun.

"Mister Earth, you're up next," said Mister Sun. "How are things?"

"I'm too popular," said Mister Earth. "From space, my colors are beautiful shades of blue, green, and gold. That's good, but with all the attention I get, everybody recognizes me and I have **no privacy**! Plus, my planet is the only one in the Solar System that is known to support life. I have almost eight billion people on my planet. It gets so **busy** here!

"And do you know that 70% of me is covered by water? I don't want **that** much water around me, especially since not everyone on Earth can swim!

"I could be happier," said Mister Earth.

"I understand," said Mister Sun.

"Your turn, Mister Mars," said Mister Sun. "How are things today?"

"Not good," said Mister Mars. "I've always been called The Red Planet, but I don't like that because so many other planets have more colors than **just red**!

"I also have the highest mountains of any planet in our Solar System. In fact, one of my mountains is ***three times higher*** than the tallest mountain on Mister Earth. It's hard for me to see around all these mountains!

"I'm just not very happy, Mister Sun," said Mister Mars.

"I'm sorry to hear that," said Mister Sun.

"Let's hear from Miss Jupiter," Mister Sun said. "What's up?"

"I'm the largest planet of all - twice as big as all the other planets combined and 318 times bigger than Mister Earth," said Miss Jupiter. "In fact, I'm just **too big**! Also, I feel like my days are just **too short** because it only takes me 9 hours and 50 minutes to rotate on my axis. This is faster than any other planet!

"And I don't ever feel relaxed since I have a Great Red Spot which is actually a huge storm that's been swirling on my surface for 350 years. I think it takes away from my good looks. I wish it would disappear!

"I'm just unhappy," said Miss Jupiter.

"I hear what you're saying," said Mister Sun.

"You're next, Miss Saturn," said Mister Sun. "How are you feeling?"

"Wow," said Miss Saturn. "Where do I begin? To start, I have at least 82 moons, so many that I haven't even named all of them yet! I also rotate twice as fast as Mister Earth - so fast that my day is almost as short as Miss Jupiter - 10 hours and 39 minutes! I wish I could slow down my rotation so I can enjoy my scenery a little more. By the way, that ring around me is **always** in the way. It follows me **everywhere** I go!

"I just wish I could be happier," Miss Saturn said.

"Well, well," said Mister Sun.

"You're next, Mister Uranus," Mister Sun said. "How are you today?"

"Actually, not well," said Mister Uranus. "Since my winters last 21 years, I'm the coldest planet in the Solar System and I can **always** see my breath! My atmosphere also has a gas called hydrogen sulfide, which makes my planet smell like rotten eggs! It's also hard for me to keep track of my 27 moons - they're **everywhere!** And I really don't like my ring. It's not very bright and doesn't look right. I want it to surround me horizontally like Miss Saturn, **not vertically**!

"I'm just not very happy," said Mister Uranus.

"Okay," said Mister Sun. "I hear you."

"Go ahead, Mister Neptune," said Mister Sun. "You're next."

"Since I'm the most distant planet in the Solar System," said Mister Neptune, "I feel so alone and far away from everyone. I also have the **strongest storms** of any planet, with my winds sometimes blowing 400 miles per hour! Although my friend Mister Uranus is the coldest planet, I'm not far behind. My temperatures are **three times lower** than the coldest places on Mister Earth. I can't stop shivering!

"It's dark and I feel alone out here," said Mister Neptune. "I'm not happy either."

Mister Sun sighed and took a deep breath. "I see," he said.

"Last, but not least, it's your turn Mister Pluto," said Mister Sun.

"Well," said Mister Pluto, "there's a lot against me. I'm not even a ***real*** planet anymore. I'm now called a Dwarf Planet because of my strange rotation and orbit. You see, I rotate on my side and my orbit is not in a circle like the other planets. But when I ***was*** a planet, I was the smallest. That's why other planets would make fun of me. Sometimes, that would hurt my feelings!

"I don't feel like I'm part of the Solar System anymore," said Mister Pluto. "This makes me feel sad and unwanted."

"I understand," said Mister Sun.

Mister Sun didn't want an Unhappy Solar System. Once he heard all of the complaints coming from his planets, he knew just what to say.

For a moment, Mister Sun dimmed his bright rays of light and asked each planet to look at him and listen carefully to his words.

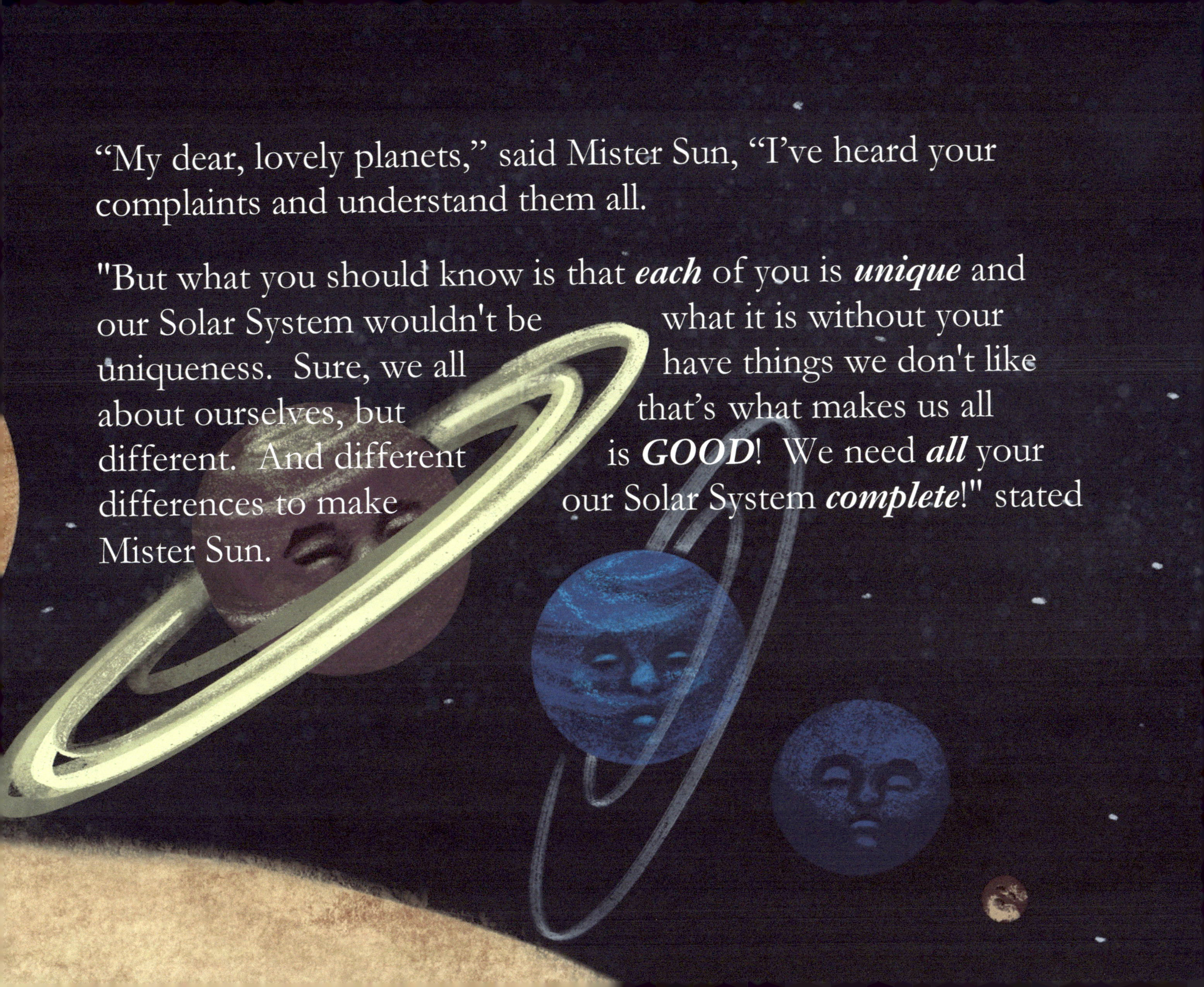

"My dear, lovely planets," said Mister Sun, "I've heard your complaints and understand them all.

"But what you should know is that *each* of you is *unique* and our Solar System wouldn't be what it is without your uniqueness. Sure, we all have things we don't like about ourselves, but that's what makes us all different. And different is *GOOD*! We need *all* your differences to make our Solar System *complete*!" stated Mister Sun.

When he finished, Mister Sun brightened his rays of light and warmed his planets like they had never been warmed before. All the planets suddenly turned their frowns into smiles, nodded their heads, and started looking at each other differently. They seemed to understand.

"You're right, Mister Sun. We are **all** unique and different!
But that's what makes us who we are. And that's **GOOD**!"
shouted the planets.

And so next time when the sun is shining brightly on your face, look up to the sky, and you will feel Mister Sun's wisdom. He understands the **GOODNESS** of every one of us and how we make our world a better place because of who we are.

About the Author
A native of California, Lorene Walker is a retired third and fourth grade educator in Omaha Public Schools. Well-known as a teacher with compassion and warmth, Lorene has always held the positive development of children close to her heart. This project is Lorene's first children's book as she looks forward to sharing future stories with her young audience. She lives with her husband in Omaha, Nebraska.

About the Illustrator
Addison Green is an artist and illustrator based in Colorado. *The Unhappy Solar System* is her first children's book and she loves the process of bringing words to life with pictures. She taught art at Fountain Valley School in Colorado Springs for twelve years, but can now be found road tripping around the United States with her dog, Stella, collecting new words and stories to put pictures to.

9 781915 424730